Robots

Experts on child reading levels
have consulted on the level of text and
concepts in this book.

At the end of the book is a "Look Back and Find" section
which provides additional information and encourages
the child to refer back to previous pages
for the answers to the questions posed.

Angela Grunsell trained as a teacher in 1969.
She has a Diploma in Reading and Related Skills
and for the last five years has advised London
teachers on materials and resources.
She works for the ILEA as an advisory teacher in
primary schools in Hackney, London.

Published in the United States in 1984 by
Franklin Watts, 387 Park Avenue South, New York, NY 10016

© Aladdin Books Ltd/Franklin Watts

Designed and produced by
Aladdin Books Ltd, 70 Old Compton Street, London W1
ISBN 0 531 04900 0
Library of Congress Catalog
Card Number: 84 51809
Printed in Belgium

FRANKLIN · WATTS · FIRST · LIBRARY

Robots

by
Kate Petty

Consultant
Angela Grunsell

Illustrated by
Mike Saunders and Adam Willis

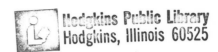

Franklin Watts
London · New York · Toronto · Sydney

What is a robot?
It is a machine that is
controlled by a computer.
Robots are programmed to do jobs.

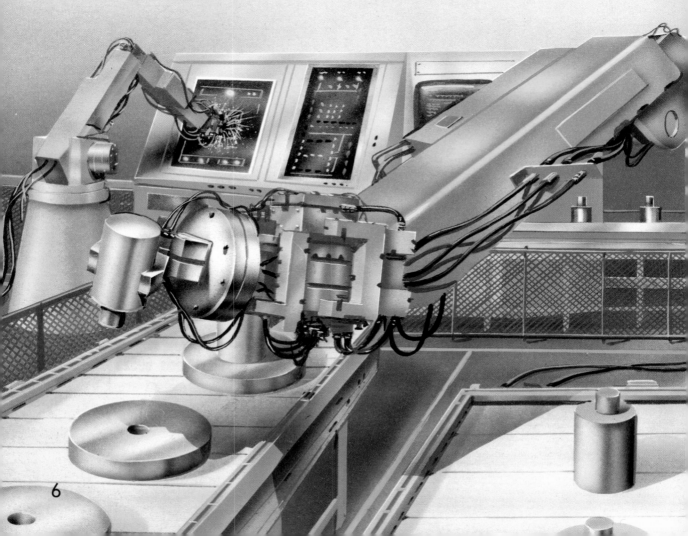

Most robots at work look like this.
They never get tired
and they never get bored.

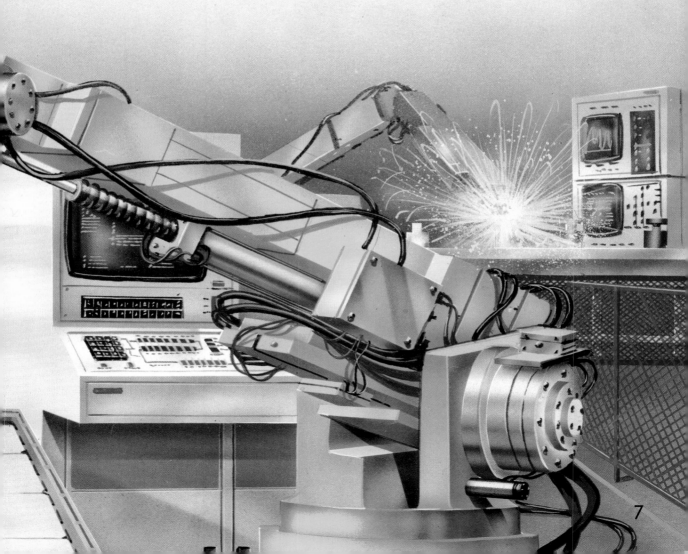

Armdroid is a little robot arm.
It has a shoulder, an elbow,
a wrist and a hand.
The computer works as the robot's brain.

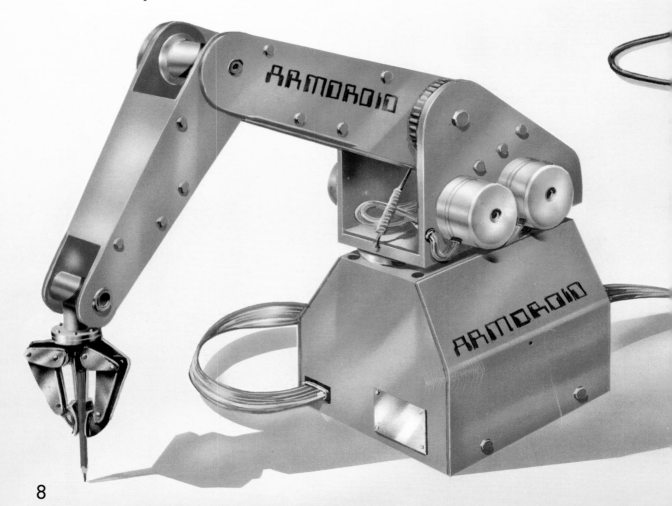

You tell the computer what you want
the robot to do by pressing the keys.
The computer controls the motors
that drive the robot arm.

Most factory robots work like a very strong arm.
They stay fixed to the ground. They can lift
heavy weights or hold a tool to work with.
This one is working with a welding torch.

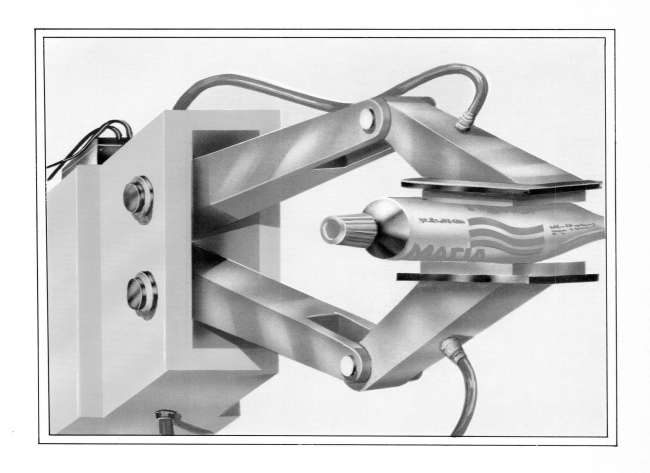

How does a robot hand – or gripper – hold
things? The "touch" sensors on these grippers
are controlled by the computer. The computer
works out how tightly the object should be held.

This robot is learning how to paint a chair.
As the operator sprays the chair the
movements of the arm are recorded by the
computer.

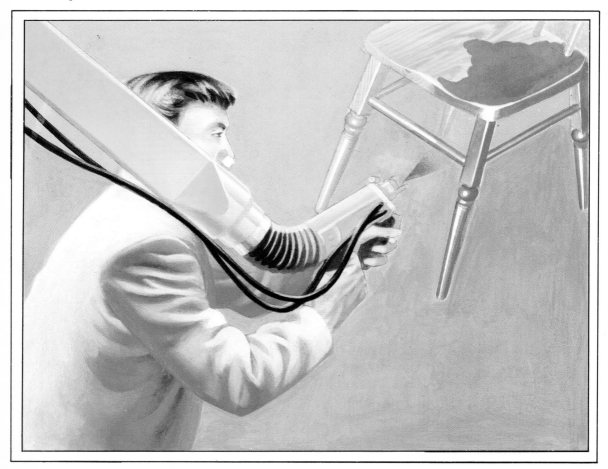

The instructions are stored on a floppy disk.
Now the robot can paint chairs by itself
whenever the disk is slotted
into the computer.

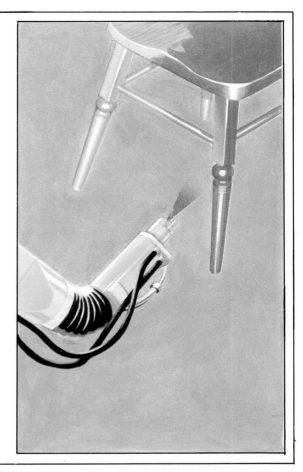

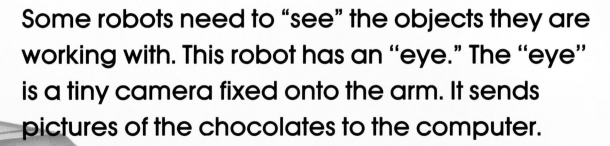

Some robots need to "see" the objects they are working with. This robot has an "eye." The "eye" is a tiny camera fixed onto the arm. It sends pictures of the chocolates to the computer.

The computer compares the pictures with the ones already in its memory. It helps the robot find a chocolate, pick it up the right way around and put it in the correct place.

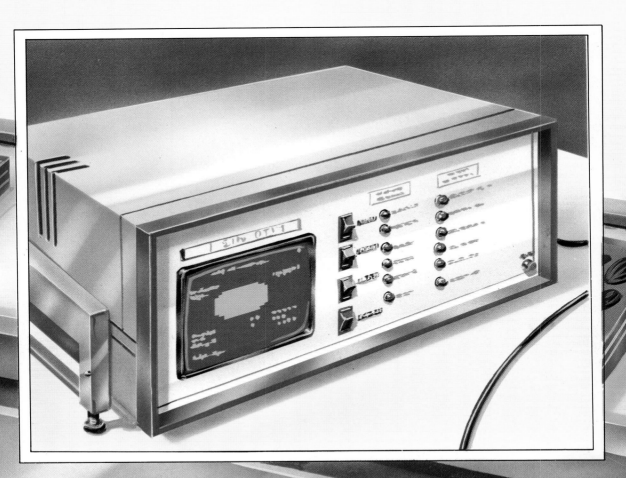

These are mobile robots. Bigtrak
is a children's toy but it is a real robot.
It carries a simple computer on board.
You tell it where to go by pressing the keys.

These robot trucks carry parts
around a car factory.
They are programmed to follow tracks
that are in the factory floor.

Hero moves by itself. It needs a different
sort of "sight" to stop it bumping into things.
It uses sonar sensors – in the same way that
a bat does – to tell if anything is in its path.

Mobile robots move on wheels, or sometimes caterpillar tracks. One which could climb stairs would need to have legs. A robot needs at least four legs to walk without falling over.

Space will always be a dangerous place for
human beings. This mobile robot was used
for exploring the Moon. It traveled
23 miles and took thousands of photographs.

Two Viking landers parachuted onto Mars after an 11-month journey from Earth. Their mechanical arms scooped up some soil. They tested it to see if there was anything living on the planet.

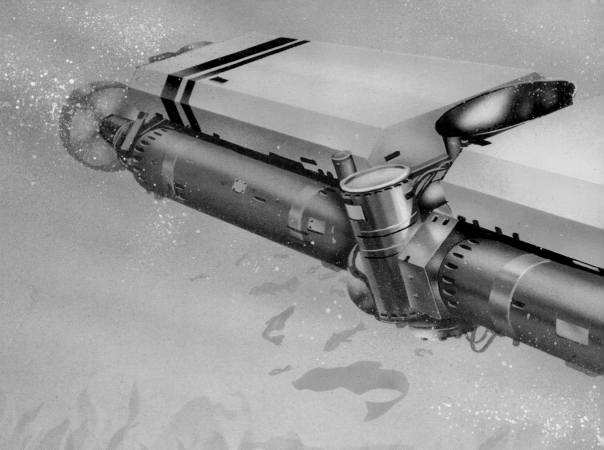

Can you think of some other places
that are not very safe for humans?
Some robots are used underwater.
They are worked by remote control.

It is difficult to send signals through water.
Now robots are being made that can work
on their own. This one will swim underwater
checking pipelines on the seabed.

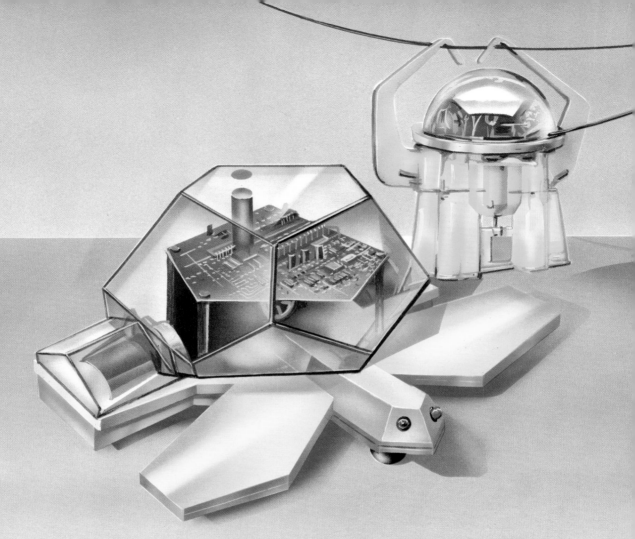

You can learn about robots by playing with them.
The Turtle is controlled from the micro. They are
linked with infrared sensors instead of a cable.
It will draw a shape if you tell it where to go.

24

The little monkey has to be constructed from a kit. It climbs along the string when you clap your hands. This working robot has been built from LEGO bricks. It is controlled from the micro too.

Topo is a personal robot.
It has been programmed to talk and sing,
carry coats or even bring you a snack.

Tot is another personal robot. It listens
for burglars as it patrols the house.
It can help with the housework too.
What jobs would you like a robot to do for you?

Look back and find

What does the Armdroid look like?

How does a robot "understand" the computer?
*The "interface" acts as a translator. It
translates the signals from the computer
into on-off signals to the robot's motors.*

What jobs can you do with your arms?

What jobs might be done by robots in a factory?

What is this one doing?

What sort of robot is this?

How does it move around?

Where do these robots work?
*They are part of the Robogate system
at the Fiat car factory in Italy.*

What are your five senses?

How does Hero "see"?
Sonar sensors work out how far away an object is by bouncing sound off it. This is like shouting in a tunnel and waiting for the echo.

Why are robots used to help us find out about space?

What is this mobile robot called?

Can you find the cameras?

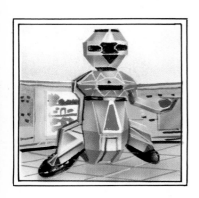

How does a robot talk and sing?
It has a voice synthesizer. It can be programmed to make noises which sound like words and tunes.

Can a robot understand what you are saying?
So far, robots have only been programmed to recognize a few simple words.

Index